MW01167020

POWER TEXT

ISBN: 978-0-9908419-2-0

Published and printed in the United States of America by Main Street Ministries.
Cover and interior design by Tracy Watkins, Inspired Studios Creative. For more information contact:

Main Street Ministries
P.O. Box 810
Pella, IA 50219

To purchase additional copies of this book or other Main Street Ministries resources go to: www.msministry.org

This book is dedicated to all the busy workers who make time each day to spend with their true supervisor.

ACKNOWLEDGMENTS

The expression of thanks that I have in my heart cannot be adequately expressed. Without the Lord speaking there would be no journal and I am overwhelmed with His love towards His servant. I thank God first for His voice that never stops loving me.

He expressed His care for me by bringing Cliff into my life many years ago. Cliff has walked beside me with his editing turned on. God has smothered my words with His love, but I do not always articulate them as such. Thank you Cliff for hearing God when language becomes a barrier for me. Thank you Cliff for listening to the voice of God with me by taking our words and expressing His heart for His people.

Bless you Tracy for allowing space in your busy life to walk with Main Street Ministries. My heart is filled with gratitude for your design and layout of this journal. Your hand of design is filled with the Spirit, for which I thank God. You have been given eyes to see what God is seeing. May your heart be richly and abundantly blessed.

Bless you faith leader for being the servant of God which impacts the workplace internationally.

INTRODUCTION

This journal has been inspired with the hope of meeting you where you are. When we are ready to hear what God is saying He is ready to speak. Each page has a daily power text message, and these messages have been sent out via text message for several years. They are messages I have received as I have learned to listen to the voice of God. Not every day has been easy but worth the wait as I wait to hear the message for the day. It has been a challenge as I waited, but they have been a part of my journey that has made many changes in my heart. I pray they do the same for you.

There's nothing better than grabbing your favorite chair and spending time listening to the Lord. Listening with the expectation to hear His still small voice is what I pray you experience. Listening with ears that are open to hear the voice of God. He desires to speak and for His people to listen. Be still is the challenge we face in a busy world and business and noise are no excuse. His voice speaks louder than any noise in this world when He is dwelling on the inside.

This is a challenge for most of us. We have stopped recognizing the voice of God because it has been drowned out by other voices that seem to scream at us. God does not scream but He speaks as a gentlemen. When we sit before Him in anticipation to hear we will hear from Him. When we open the word of God and delight ourselves in Him we will hear from Him. He will speak when we learn to turn off the distractions that are in our way and focus on the quietness of His voice.

Do not give up because you do not hear Him the first time or even the second but keep pressing in to His throne room. The distractions become less when we press through the noise. Try not to persuade the noise to be silent but press through the noise to hear the voice of God. Try not to allow emotion or frustration to rule but recognize that it is a simple emotion that tries to detour your way towards God. Allow the truth of God's word to guide your mind and heart as you make your way toward Him.

"Come to me, all you who are weary and burdened, and I will give you rest." (Matthew 11:28)

The invitation is to come. To come to the Lord filled with anticipation and haste longing to see and hear what He has to say. Longing to be loved and allow your burdens to be released. He offers rest as you make your way towards Him. Do not grow weary but keep going—He is waiting.

POWER TEXT

by

Sabra & Cliff Dyas

FAITH MOVES

Faith moves into the heart and out through your hands, feet, and mouth. If faith doesn't move it becomes lifeless.

THE GREAT PHYSICIAN

Jesus said healthy people don't need a doctor—sick people do. His prescriptions were written in blood. Allow Jesus to meet your needs. (Matthew 9:12-13)

FREEDOM

God in His perfect love gave us the freedom to choose. Real love gives others the freedom of choice.

REFUGE

Keep me safe, oh God, for I have come to you for refuge. (Psalms 16:1) God is our safe place in a troubled world. Allow Him to comfort you.

WAKE WITH THANKFULNESS

STOP . . . right where you are and just start thinking of all God's blessings he has given you—we cannot out-bless our heavenly father. Try every morning the rest of the week to just start thanking God right when you open your eyes. (Ephesians 5:18-21)

THE RIGHT PATH

The shortest route is not always the wisest route. Sometimes God will reroute our journey to protect us. (Genesis 13:17-18)

COMPLAINING

Complaining is a trap that will constantly give you more to complain about. Release and bring yourself before God, who can satisfy your needs.

LIGHTEN UP

Persevering requires us to throw off the weights that are holding us back. What is holding you back? Don't give up—get lighter.

PLAN AHEAD

Make a commitment now before you make choices later.

YOU ARE UNIQUE

There is only ONE you created by the architect's hands. Allow His hands to continue to shape you into His design!

BE LOVED FIRST

Love starts by receiving God's true love for you and then giving His love to others. Receive His true love today.

SERVE

The Lord has washed your feet; you should wash the feet of others. Who can you serve?

BE SOMETHING NEW

God is doing new and creative works all the time. Be a part it and allow Him to use you for something new. New wine calls for new wineskins. (Mark 2:22)

STRENGTH TO LOVE

Lord, we praise you. Lord, we ask for you to continue to release your grace and gifts over your children. Give us strength to serve you by loving others. Forgive us when we desire to see our country change and sit by passively. Give us your desire to feed and clothe the poor. Give us your weeping eyes for our country. In Jesus' name, amen!

STORMS

Life will have storms but it is what we do in them that will help us grow. Allow Jesus the room to grow in you. He can silence the storm.

THE HEAD OF THE CHURCH

God has given all authority to Christ and made him the head of the church. The position of power has been taken and we submit. (Ephesians 1:22)

DO WHAT?

"What do you want me to do for you?" asked Jesus. (Mark 10:51) Jesus is still asking. How will you answer?

TEACH

Teach where you have been touched.
Where has God touched you?

OUR CONTRACT

God's word is a binding contract bought with blood. Do you need words of truth for your life? The agreement has already been signed. Receive!

PEOPLE OF HOPE

No worries today—there is more to come. Stay tuned. We are people who have a hope and future!

DADDY

We have a daddy in heaven who knows our story. His desire is to be a part of our story. He desires you. What do you need from your daddy?

SPEAK

Church-God is making his appeal through us. Bricks don't speak, people do. Let your voice be His wherever He finds you.

LIGHT IN THE DARKNESS

Speaking the truth in love is like turning on the light in a dark room. Shed some light today.

A BIG GOD

Our God will do what He promised to do. Live today fully convinced in His ability. What have you seen God do lately?

PERSPECTIVE

Things aren't always what they seem. Need a new perspective? Look up.

MEASURES

We can become obsessed with measuring our own moral muscle but forget to put it into practice in real life. Make sure your measures don't outweigh your practice.

LET GO

Some things must be put away in order to grow up. If you keep holding on they will hold you back. What's holding you back? (I Peter 2:1-2)

STRENGTH IN WEAKNESS

When we fall short we always have someone taller beside us. His strength is perfected in our weakness.

HELP DESK

Need direction? There is a help desk waiting for all who are needy and humble of heart. He who sits there is more than able.

LOVE & POWER

When the power of love becomes more important than the love of power we find the purpose we were called to fulfill.

VISION

As a faith leader because of your unity with Christ you can walk this day seeing life and people through His eyes. Ask for His vision today and be prepared for an adventure.

MY RESIGNATION

Serving in the Kingdom of God is not a popularity contest. It is a resignation of my status at the King's feet.

GOD'S-EYE VIEW

Faith leaders, look up. Don't be consumed with what you can see in the natural. Ask God for His view and see His Kingdom released.

NEED

Jesus paid the price for our deepest needs. He is the answer to all we need. What do you need? Seek Him first.

LIGHT IN THE STORM

Even behind the clouds of the worst storms light remains.

THE ENEMY'S FEAR

We have an enemy who fears what you might become. However, don't fear, because You are desperately loved and accepted by the One who has overcome the enemy. Receive.

LIFE AND BREATH

Take a deep breath today asking God to fill you with His life and breathe for you. Now you are ready to exhale His life to the world.

LOVE DESTROYS FEAR

There is no fear in love. But perfect love drives out fear, because fear has to do with punishment. (Ephesians 4:18) We all have fears. No matter what your job title, degree, salary, or status we all have fear.

ACCEPTANCE

The ruler in the Kingdom we serve showed His acceptance of You by going to the cross. That's the Kingdom you work in today.

A FAITHFUL GUIDE

A GPS can only guide your path here and has an annoying voice. God can speak and guide your path on an adventure of a lifetime. Let Him lead.

LEAVE THE PAST BEHIND

Jesus leads us beyond blaming others for our condition. He leads us in leaving the past behind and walking with Him in fullness.

SHINE

Light up everywhere you go today by letting the Holy Spirit shine through you. Let everything you do reflect Him.

OBEDIENCE

What if obedience to God is the purpose for all you do today?

GIVING

A faith leader's decision to give starts in their heart. If the heart is filled with greed, the giving will only be to the self.

INTEGRITY

If you have integrity you are the same no matter where you are or who you are with. You get to sign your name at the end of the day.

RELEASE

If you walk in disappointments, they will hold you captive. Give them to the ONE who cares and He will release you.

SPIRITUAL STRATEGY

A faith leader applies strategy that first started with the chief strategists. He knows how to defeat the enemy's tactics.

MEETING NEEDS

A faith leader sees the needs of others and is willing to meet them. What are you willing to do?

FAILURE & SUCCESS

Dying on a cross was a sign of failure. Don't let the world define failure for you. What looks like failure can be your success.

DECIDE TO LOVE

The decision to love others begins with you, not them. Don't wait for others to show love.

WHAT DO YOU VALUE?

What you are saying yes and no to are a clear indication of what you value. Ask yourself, does your yes and no clearly align with what you value?

LOYALTY

Loyalty gives undivided attention to the heart. Loyalty remains when betrayal is offered. Be sensitive to the offers of betrayal today.

24 HOURS

We all have the same 24 hours but we will achieve different results. What are the results the Holy Spirit is after? Allow Him 24 hours.

DRIVING FORCE

A faith leader's vision is so God compelling that they are driven by vision, not ego. What drives you?

LIKE A CHILD

The Lord looks forward to us calling out to Him just as a child to their parent. He desires for you to always turn to Him. He is waiting.

FREEDOM TO CHOOSE

God gives us the freedom to choose. What decisions will you make today that will set you free?

TO NOT FORGIVE

When we choose not to forgive we are giving our heart to the offender. Protect your heart. Forgive!

PROBLEMS

Problems are opportunities for God's wisdom to speak.

WITHOUT YOUR PERMISSION

There's a lot of competition after your heart, whether good or evil. Neither one can have your heart without your permission.

AGREEMENT

God's purpose for you is to give you a satisfying and rich life. Allow your decisions to agree with His purpose.

ECHOES

God's voice is not locked behind the walls of our church buildings . . . His voice is echoing in the hallways of our workplace.

Stillness before God empowers movement with God.

BE STILL AND MOVE

THE PRODUCT OF WAITING

God is able to do whatever He promises to do. Waiting on the promise produces a product . . . faith.

RESPECT

Respect yourself. Christ showed you respect all the way to the cross.

HEAVEN REALITIES

A faith leader can see the potential of what God can do by looking to heaven realities. Thy Kingdom come on earth as it is in heaven.

IMAGINATION

Imagination is a place where God expands vision. Will you let Him expand yours?

RELEASE GRACE

People would rather be loved than judged. When we love we release God's grace.

GLORIFY SHAMELESSLY

There's no shame in our story. It's to bring God glory. We don't have to save face when our purpose is to glorify God.

STAND

Staying true to the word of God is conviction. Standing in your convictions even if you are alone is integrity. Will you stand today?

SPIRITUAL PORTFOLIO

Your net worth is not determined by your financial portfolio; it has already been determined by the cross.

GENEROSITY

Practicing generosity comes when you understand how rich you are in Christ. Will you practice being rich today?

DEFINE SUCCESS

How you define success will determine who you are trying to please. What's your definition?

ANCHORED

Keeping anchored to the truth will keep you from drifting away. What are you anchored to?

COMPLAINING

Every time we complain about the church we really are complaining about people. Take your complaints to the One who changes hearts. Yours first.

ACCEPT

When you begin to see yourself as God does you will see others as He does. Do you struggle to accept others? His grace is sufficient.

The vote is in—God is still in control!

GOD IN CHARGE

CELEBRATE

God isn't tolerating you—He is celebrating you. Surround yourself with those who are celebrating you.

God can see you right now and loves who He sees. No need to hide.

STOP HIDING

THE UNSEEN

If you need evidence for everything you do, you will stay in one place for a long time. Now faith is the substance of things hoped for, the evidence of things not seen. (Hebrews 11:1)

NON-STOP LOVE

Love is more than a feeling because when it hurts love doesn't stop. God's love doesn't ever stop for you.

20/20 VISION

Faith is the lens that allows you to see beyond what is visible. What lens will you see through today?

ACCOUNTABLE

Show someone how much you love them today by holding them accountable because someday at the knee of Jesus we will bow.

BELIEF AND ACTIONS

Who you choose to believe in today will determine your actions. Belief and actions will work together. What are your actions saying?

Every page of your story has the opportunity to empower someone's faith. What page will you share today?

YOUR STORY

WORDS OF LIFE

God's word in the beginning brought life. His words still create life. Will you allow His words to speak life today?

GOD'S HANDS

God's promises are His hands opening up to you. Instead of taking matters into your own hands wait on God's hands.

RESCUE

There is no power God can't rescue you from. Do you need a lion's mouth shut today?

MOUNTAINS

Faith overcomes what you can't see because of the mountains you can see. What mountains do you need moved?

NEEDS

The needs of others give us an opportunity to reveal the love God has given us.

Your King has given you a sword to use in His Kingdom to fight off the predators. Are you using it?

THE SWORD

YOUR ASSIGNMENT

Have a conference call with your king and receive a Kingdom assignment. He's waiting for you.

LOVE TRUTH

Loving the truth is like loving freedom. You can't have freedom without truth. Find some in the word today.

STAND STRAIGHT

Stand up straight with your head held high by allowing God to shoulder all that would weigh you down. He is able!

LOOK UP

The concerns of this world can keep your heart and head down. Look up and receive a perspective that is not of this world.

THE SHEPHERD

Wouldn't it be refreshing to be led beside quiet waters by our shepherd who restores our emptiness? Oh wait! Be still. You are!

Pride says I. Humility says we.

FROM ME TO WE

IMPORTANCE

When you allow God to show you how important you are to Him you won't have to waste time trying to convince others how important you are!

WAITING

God isn't waiting for me to disappoint Him so He can discipline me. He disciplines me because I failed to wait on Him.

THE KNOCK

Someone needs to get the door. He stands and knocks waiting to spend time with you! Will you answer?

THE ARTIST

When we take God out of the picture how can we expect Him to be the artist? When we take the pen away how can He be the author?

ZAPPED

Has your enthusiasm and strength been zapped? You've been unplugged. Plug into the ALL POWERFUL and find unlimited resources in strength.

THE GIFT OF PEACE

Peace is a present Jesus left for us. Unwrap it and find contentment that is beyond this world. It is His presence.

VISION

Without vision people perish. Without God's vision we would have perished. How do you respond to His vision?

PRESENCE

All the presents in the world could not replace the presence of Jesus. Thank you God for sending your Son. May His presence fill your day.

STAR STRUCK

There are 1 followed by 24 zeros stars in the universe, and the Lord calls them all by name. His power is beyond our understanding. Will you bow under His Authority?

GOD IS GOOD

Having faith isn't about striving to be good enough. It's about trusting God who is good enough and His goodness working in you!

THE NAME

Practice worship by calling on the name of Jesus. Praise His name and all darkness will flee. Do you need some light?

WORK IS A GIFT

If a world doesn't work . . . it doesn't work. Work is a gift God has given. Just think if the garbage men decided not to work. Every person doing their part! What's yours?

THE JOURNEY

Don't wait till you meet the goal to enjoy. The journey along the way to meeting the goal is the goal. Enjoy!

THE INGREDIENTS

If you don't like the results you are getting from life try adding a different ingredient. Love, forgiveness, and selflessness—just to name a few.

GRACE IS THERE

Grace is there for the grass beneath your feet not for the grass on the other side of the fence.

TRAVEL LIGHT

You don't need to take your suitcase along when following Jesus. The only requirement is you. What's holding you back?

Wisdom gives you the opportunity to get paid beyond six figures. It offers joy in doing what is true and right. Look for it today and get paid.

TRUTH'S EMBRACE

When we stumble we have a God who holds us up with truth before we fall. Allow truth to embrace you.

TRUST & CONFIDENCE

Trusting in God will give you confidence in yourself. Who do you trust today?

DECEPTION

Deception is the baton that is passed when truth stops. Win in life by running the race with truth.

THE GAME

When we use people like chess pieces it won't take long for them to see the game and then we have lost what's most important. PEOPLE!

Here I am send (<u>name</u>). Are you willing to be used by God today? He is willing.

SENT

MOVE

When we know God—the battle is nearly over. The next step is to move in the know.

TIME WELL SPENT

Jesus showed what was important with His time by healing the sick and sharing the Gospel . . . how will you use your time?

GIVE COURAGE

What words will you use today to impart courage to someone along the way? You are a gift God has given to this world.

Don't wait until your life is at its end to start living. Live every day to the fullest.

START NOW

WAKE UP

We start living life to the full when our hearts are awakened to the people around us. Who can you serve today?

MULTIPLY TIME

Do you need more time in your day? Spend time with the ONE who has the answers. He did a lot in seven days.

RAISE THE BAR

Maturity will raise the bar and the Holy Spirit will empower us to reach it.

BUILD WISELY

If you are confident, you are building others. If you are arrogant, you are building self. Who could you build up today?

MASTERPIECE

The picture God has in His mind of you is a masterpiece. Will you give Him the paintbrush?

STRONG ARMS

There isn't any situation that God's arm can't reach. His arm is not too short. Where do you need the touch of God today?

THE WILL

The apple wasn't evil—it was the will. The will is where we meet the Gospel power.

Kingdom vision will challenge your will. Will you leave your nets and follow?

LEAVE YOUR NETS

THINKING

Want to know what God is thinking?
His thoughts came alive in Jesus.

EVERYDAY PURPOSE

Love can't be contained to a day. It's the purpose of everyday. Be a day ahead of the calendar; show love today.

THE MOTIVE OF LOVE

Jesus had no motive other than love. When your motives become love you find purpose. The love of Jesus took him to the feet of His disciples.

MOVE IN FAITH

Faith is assured of what God says is true . . . obedience is moving in faith. Where do you need to move today?

BLAMELESS

God didn't point His finger at you in blame. He brought Jesus who took all the blame. Will you receive?

GIFTS & TALENTS

Gifts and talents are from God, and every time we use them for His glory we advance His Kingdom. Will you use yours for Him today?

SHOW JESUS

Allowing God to use you allows God to show Jesus at work.

Weakness is a doorway for God's strength to make His way in. Welcome Him in.

STRENGTH IN WEAKNESS

BE MISSED

Live your life so that when you are gone even the undertaker is sad.

MOMENT BY MOMENT

We don't have grace to worry. We have grace when we walk moment by moment with our God.

BREATHE LIFE

His presence will bring fullness to your day as He breathes in life.

Prayer reaches where we can't.

MEASURE UP

There is no measurement for the love of God, except unending and unfailing.

HOME AWAY FROM HOME

Placing your hope here will make your heart sick. Look toward your eternal home and you will find eternal hope.

THANKFUL PEACE

Peace is promoted with thankfulness. What are you thankful for today?

Troubles come and when they do we have Jesus who stands there with arms open wide and says take heart, I have overcome.

THE OVERCOMER

PROVISION

Your Father is loving you and providing for you even if you feel like you are in a dry and weary place. Look up—there is manna.

LIVE ETERNAL

Seeing life from an eternal perspective allows you to live to the fullest. Be prepared every day to live.

EXCESSIVE PRAYER

Be aware excessive praying can change the way you do life. Do you need a change?

LIGHTEN UP

Need to lose some weight? Pull up a chair and sit with the Father and walk away lighter.

PAID IN FULL

The price of God's love has already been paid. We just need to pick it up.

THE FORCE OF TIME

Time is a force that makes relationships strong. Will you choose to take time to show someone you care?

Love moves our heart to greater work!

THE LORD OF PEACE

Where the Lord is there is peace. Where do you need peace? Invite Him there.

WAKE UP

The alarm is going off for Christians everywhere to wake up and serve. Are you hitting the snooze button? You may not have another minute.

DEFINITIONS

You have been defined by God. How do you define yourself? Looking for significance in any other place will lead to that place defining you.

YOUR STORY

The story God knows about you is the one you proclaim before others and the one you fear others will see. No need to fear—God loves you.

NO PITY

We can sit and complain about all the wrong and have a pity party or we can live our faith and help fix the wrong.

POSITIVE I.D.

Being the person the Lord has called you to be will keep you from becoming what the world says you should be.

Pay close attention—God has something He wants you to do today.

WATCH & LISTEN

NEARNESS

Draw near to God and He will draw near to you.

TRUTH & LIGHT

Without truth there is only darkness. Speak truth and watch the light appear.

SEAL OF APPROVAL

You are "God approved."

GOOD GOSSIP

Be a reverse gossip. Applaud people behind their back.

NO RESPECT

Sin has no respect for you.

GENEROSITY

Being generous shows the world that God is listening to our prayers. Who can you show generosity to today?

CLEAN UP

Uncluttering the mind will allow more space for God. Create some space for God—take out the trash.

THE DEBT

God doesn't foreclose on us because we can't pay our debt to Him . . . He already paid and we live debt free in His Kingdom.

HEAVY TOPIC

When the weight of this world becomes too heavy remember God carries His people.

NO BETTER

The temptation is to think you are better than others. The sin is to act on it.

LEAD WISELY

Leading people to Jesus will keep you from leading them to yourself.

FOLLOW & LEAD

Depending on who you follow will determine how far you can lead others.

PROJECTION

The image you project to your workplace will determine what you want them to believe about you.

OBSTACLES

Let us draw near to the throne room of God to find what we should do today, and let us confess all that keeps us from doing it.

FIND COURAGE

Often when we are the most uncomfortable is when great opportunity comes for new God courage.

IN HIS HANDS

Take a look in the sky today and become aware of who holds it. Be thankful it is not spinning out of control.

JOY EVERLASTING

God leads us away from things that once brought temporal joy so we can find everlasting joy.

GETTING GREAT

God is making us something beyond ourselves. He is making us into something greater than we are in the present.

GET FIT

Faith is the exercise we do that makes us fit for God. When we lead with faith we exercise. As a faith leader exercise your faith—it will make you fit for God.

THE SOLUTION

Not knowing what to do in a difficult situation is not the problem. The problem is not knowing where to go to find the solution. Faith shows you that God has a solution to your problem.

OUR BEST

God met us at our worst and made us to be at our best with Him.

BE FREE

When we choose Jesus we no longer have to obey sin. Jesus set us free from the power of sin in our lives.

RIGHT MIND

Having a mind set on doing right will keep you from doing wrong.

THANKS

Contentment is not found in the future. It begins today when we begin to thank God. What are you thankful for?

GRATITUDE ATTITUDE

We are not prepared for the future until we live today in gratitude.

HEROES

We need to celebrate the real heroes of this world. The ones who do what is right even when it costs them.

SHOW UP

Be silent no more—live your faith out loud! Let someone know they matter to God by showing up in their life with the love of Jesus.

NO MARGINS

Keep the Gospel off the margins.
Bring it into the middle of your life and
you will experience its power.

SEEK

Form a habit today of continually seeking God's presence.

NO SITTING

God did not save us to sit us. We were created to be active for God, so be careful not to become deactivated.

MIRROR

You were made in the image of God and designed to reflect Him to the world.

TIME TO TURN?

When considering making a change take the time to take your foot off of the accelerator of life and prayerfully consider the turn.

TO DO

God knows why we do what we do and yet leads us to do what He has created us to do.

PROVEN

God loved you even before you tried to prove yourself to the world.

CLOSED DOORS

Sin may call out to you behind a closed door, but you are no longer obligated to answer the door. You have been given power to ignore its call.

DEEP

The deep love of God moves us away from all that is shallow.

FULFILLMENT

We need to forgive each other for not being God. Only God can fulfill your deepest longings.

OVERCOMING

When confronted with difficulties faith will lead you to overcome. Complaining will lead you to being overcome.

CPSIA information can be obtained at www.ICGtesting.com
Printed in the USA
LVOW04*2337071015

457289LV00008B/16/P

9 780990 841920